Blurring The Flaws of
PERFEKTION

Keith A. Mandella

Wasteland Press
Louisville, KY USA
www.wastelandpress.com

Blurring The Flaws of Perfektion
by Keith A. Mandella

Front cover image based on
an original drawing by RPM

First Printing – February, 2004

ISBN: 1-932852-02-6

Printed in the U.S.A.

For Pilar, whose Inspiration, Support, Love and Dedication soars Beyond the present and far into the Unknown, Ever-after.

For that I am Grateful beyond words and remain Forever in your Spiritual debt...All my Love is yours.

INTRODUCTION / FAST FORWARD

I have always believed the best form of entertainment media is porn. Why? Because you can't give away the ending. You know it already.

I write this in good faith, in the 'now'. But you, the reader, is enveloped in these sinister pages long after the initial primal etchings were constructed and later, misconstrued. I plead in sincere hope that at press time and the micro-kinetic periods of worship there-after, that my feelings and obtuse points of view will have remained undaunted and seemingly impeccable as to the harsh standards I have established since first embarking on this hound crazy excursion.

So let the cracked brass bells ring and sing the funeral march to the dreams! Give the astrophysicists the needed and necessary data to prove the 'Big Bang Theory'. Take into consideration the potential damage to the Earth's magnetic field. Do not forget the tidal waves and various uncontrollable fits and disasters of immense cosmic proportion to follow. Let us not forget the destruction in its unfathomable wake resulting in massive rifts in space and time. Let us not forget ...

'So shake your ass in wild abandon as the Earth burns around us in that sweet Chernobyl glow. Huddle tight in your nitrous filled cocoon of cool and let the good times roll.'

\m/ \m/ ,
KAM

CONTENTS

Blurring the Flaws of Perfektion
Harikari with Dull Conviction
Incongruent Scattered Mind Lines
Digitus Infamus
Untitled
100% Fiction
U.T.I.
Gemini Nautilus Monolith
Strength in Numbness
Spiritual Stagnation
Drip
Biting Words
Dancing Swallow of Eternity
Dilated Truth of You
Revelations on the Hindsight
    Of the Yuletide
Too Late to Blackout
Shit Pig
Phallic Didactic
Silvertigo
Sold you my Volatile Ego
Got to Die, or You'll Live to
    Regret It
Agenda of Gabionade
Apocalyptic Drug March
Pecuniary Diluvium
Epitaph
Shards of Inspiration
Art of Shit Art
Tuesday, I Think
[M]ass-inine
Sink Like a Stone
Seraglio
Plausible Fingering
Maximum Meandering
Torrid Holiday Tomorrow Comes
Rostrum Debris Havoc
Igneous Pulchritude
7 A.M.
Election Day

Wisdom, Grasshopper
Dust Cloud
Precious Dregs
This is What Screams
  Are Made of
Thorns of Hope
Last Voice Lost
A Rope Ends It
  = Desperation
Ronson Award
The Anti-Social
  Drinker
Damaged Baggage
Ultimate Groove Cushion
Effigy
Palanquin
Postpartum Postponement
Requiem and Goodnight
Exeunt Wound Genesis

Blurring the [F]laws of Perfektion

You can't point your fingers when they're clenched into fists...
You're approaching that fifteenth level of realization of spiritual
comprehension;
You are somewhat closing in on what it is really like to be alive,
Or so it seems.
The all-encompassing need to feel utterly and completely vindicated
about your brief tenure here on Earth;
Here in this weary, fragile and ultimately forgettable vehicle of flesh
and blood...

The enemies, Alibis and murder
The exhilaration in ruin
Power - Sex and despair
Meaninglessly vague and in disrepair;
Apprehensive;
Atmospherically rambling and offensive;
Haunted, Dreamy and Distorted

Truly the final showdown of the
 Last brain cell standing...

Harikari with Dull Conviction

Virtual avalanche of guilt peppering on my head
Streaming,
  Torturous fits of depression

I stare
I see deep likeness
The visage of aborted babies in the stucco outside the
  Window;
Some have horns,
Some are asleep
All are smiling,
  Black teeth

My skills are shallow, exfoliated veneer
Too much desire to wallow and crawl away from here
Living hard;
Cracks your face and the fragile vulnerability of your
    Immunity
You feel impervious to damage, much less shut down

Upon every reverie, you reach for the peace wielding
    Facade that kills the numbness
The straining, stretching will to face it-

Harikari (*cont.*)

Some days in Hell are cold
You shake your wounded, pathetic frame 'til you retrieve
   The solace of the panacea that cuts the pretension
Cuts the mechanism that boils your resilience-
That same schism that you swear you won't climb
   Tomorrow,
The Mountain of shit that you love to perch upon,
The view and vibrant breeze sweep your head into an
Open state of Euphoric - Selective - Amnesia
You constantly cloud the passer-by apprehension and
   Treat it naive

Aggravated and alone, you face the snarling chasm;
Look down to see the jagged shale geodes and deep
   Hue of black below
The grey piercing confusion
The area between the view and your rhythmic hovering
   That you crave to dive into
And why you don't-
   That's there too...

So what?
All it equates to is recognizing the same lie every time you tell it...

Harikari (*cont.*)

And it makes you feel better
For awhile;
The hours of serenity are free from the harnessing
   Trepidation felt the rest of the day
The times you tremble and loathe and despise your
   Very existence
And you hope;
Hope, that no one ever, that you give even the slightest
   Malignant shit about, ever has to feel like this...

Incongruent Scattered Mind Lines

These incongruent scattered mind lines
That once would lie (e)motionless under shag woolen/
   Beige carpet pillars

You   refused to get it, to understand it
You   never wanted to comprehend it
You   refused to look my problems in the eye
And so did I

It wasn't the quantity, it was the concept that was the
   Demise,
Not the ingredient intoxicants, but the theme in disguise

And I'm not surprised–you suddenly realized– the
   Premonition to be king-sized

   Throttled prediction
   Harikari with Dull Conviction

On the harangue bloomed the miser,
   Poor to allotropic
Or perched near the hobo who was much too
   Philanthropic;

He claimed it vermillion, we saw it jaundice
Displeased of the prize
A second-hand version of Tijuana syphilis–

Digitus Infamis

In the barracks of mischief, the passage of guilt bends
   Too white and persistent to really believe in such
   Falsehood;
All the escape artist attempts to waste the mourning-
All the coughing, exhausted rifles gleam of flooded
   Inertia and misery of deserted prophesy-
The demons who blink and caress the crotch of bigotry
   That bang the fiery wings of Autumn away;
The tempers of heresy spit into the cauldron of
   Scrutinized trenches of ignorance;
Quickly puddling up with the burrowing, brooding
   Drowning voices-

In a wasteland of oppression,
The pillars kill and the mimes hunker in bunkers,
   Under blankets of uncertainty-
Rotting soldiers drag the dregs;
   Soon lifeless masses of graceless towering imperfection
Beckoning guilt,
Summoning blame,
We dive to the gallows of memories brothel,
Where shadows scrape bandages of clarity from the blast
   Of Destiny's furrowing, explosive eyelids

Digitus Infamis (*cont.*)

The wombs of flattery grin into the haven of disorder-
Cradling the cages of majesty and enable cankered gravity
   To swarm and float with the devotion of the eyrie ocean-
Gouging perfection;
Flowing, irrational reason
Lovingly grabbing you by the throat with a smile . . .
(Dia de la muerta of political correctness-9/11/01)

Untitled

That's the Devil's handshake
You're now on the payroll of his Rehab and Remission

The Heaviest burden is unfulfilled potential
Dormant possibilities
Cankered and pitted seemlessly;
     Propping you up for failure

And all you were is what is remembered
The fine granule residue of your reputation,
     Good or otherwise
All the ancient, classic words we freely quote and
     Nestle into
The thrown color and scorn of the Masters
Artists and painters we gaze into and marvel at-

Time is most acidic
Turning pages of our history to dust and ebbing
     Masterpieces of marble and stone to sand

My own passages and observations put to paper have
     Had at it with the elements
Not different from my predecessors, they have lost

II.
My brain is so scrambled, I'm hearing voices
Options;
Giving me choices
Ravaged in mind and in spirit
I can feel it so close, but I'm not even near it-

Scratched out revisions-
Spontaneous decisions
Trying to figure out the right...

100% Fiction (and that's a fact)

Commotions boxed in and crouching in the crevice of
   Disillusion...
Pseudo stagnant nostalgic confusion
Same shit everyday
Like being in Groundhog Day

As long as the liver can metabolize,
   I won't be ostracized
Warning shot was a hit,
   Struck between the eyes...

... all the day's frustrations just melt away
Pain tied to your years of lies,
   And the truth beheaded
Senses can take a brutal beating
Building slowly like a good fuck,
   Before the lust takes over entirely-

Darkness is comfort for a wrecked spirit-
A void that cannot be filled

Prostitution of Integrity
lying means the same to me
Sharpness of tongue is exceeded by the dullness of mind
This time...

100% Fiction (and that's a fact) (*cont.*)

As if things were getting better out East;
The granules are rushing to the bottom now,
  Faster than ever...

U.T.I.

Desperately wanting to be locked into a drug trance,
But with no finance,
It's a nuisance...

I wake in a panic
My eyes clicked open; Alive and
My dream blew into dust...

Clamoring whispers and stumbling fluidity
Mumbling in intoxicated tongues
Rambling;
Sleepwalking thru hallways of the beating sickness

Pacified to narcolepsy?
Well, let me see...

Bullets ricochet the gaze,
    Of the ever present narcotic haze-

Atmosphere is bare;
Up here
Mesmerizing with the dynamic,
    Hip-notic drone of it's own. . .

Gemini Nautilus Monolith

Your dirge is creepy and spurring and stunning and
   Sultry with junkie shivers;
Ghostly, sparse and skeletal

Into the thin
Into the shape you're in
Got to be lost, Got to begin

Like a lingering hug good night...

...Northern planets patiently reward each rain stroke of
   Time on a long lunar tingling beyond the curves of
   Crossed particular change...

Bow down to the acrylic purple god that does you no
   Good as he pinches your earlobes tightly together-
And exhausts the day away thru a horn of grey smoke;
Laughing all the opiate eyes gently to flight and
   Rapidly squeezes the pedestrian feet to sleep
   With the bull-whip-crack of daylight's swift,
   Heavy Hand . . .

. . . The moon's liquid shroud of darkness encompasses
over the sun,
I sail by;
Unnoticed

Gemini Nautilus Monolith (*cont.*)

Murmur's demise is drowned out in a pool of lateral
   Silver tears–
–So let us pummel the Mikado with lordly skivers
Upturn the deranged overlord with exhausting insular
   Plexus; Slicker and more wretched...veneous

Strength in Numbness

The tender fingertips that pull at the sinewed strings of
   My heart;
Tugs the deliberate tears that curve slowly around my
   Iris and down my temple-
The sickened heart, I've not since nursed
The cool running camouflaged prickly hairs on end-

She comes;
Like the small, angel fairy;
Down;
And she inundates me with happiness that her small
   Wings of marijuana leaves douse and scatter
   Throughout me-
My tongue drips and tastes of drug
My teeth grind in chatter with numb wanting to slowly
   Still and sedate her tongue to sleep upon mine

The bloodlines in my eyes
You can see all the tributaries flowing out to the poison
   Ocean that tells intricately of where I've been-

The tiny black clustered islands that float motionless to
   The crescendo and we push the squint to close;
Shut off;
Now completely fused as one of parts equal-

Strength ... (*cont.*)

And we sat;
We felt the walls that kept us apart crumble into sand,
   That we slowly siphoned between our toes-
Our dilated eyes gazed thru each other at the direction
   Of the fast appearing orange rising of the Sun-
And we waited...

...And the tiny hunched shoulders over the crooked
   Little appendages that smoothly splash down on the
      Ivory strains of her baby grand-
Sprinkling me with more of the soaring dirge that is
   Sure to strike ferocious effect on me over each
      Becoming chord's progression and ascension ...

Dedicated to the wonder of my life, my wife, Pilar.

Spiritual Stagnation

Blitzkrieg memories
Ashes;
Seamless, pungent, flaring nostrils
These are the days of Bummer
The harsh, windless murmurs of forgotten murder

Dots of flashless triumph
Sporadic, jabbing enlightenment
Crisp, rapier rattle
Dark, withdrawn and blinking
Aztec smoke guarded circle of infamy
Desperate, appearing pupils crowd the Crown
The Tin Empire falls;
Down,
All around,
Us

...More likely,
There was history in the morning
Colors, creatures, firm circles weave Inca salty empires
Encompassing mild men forever in error, who
Walk senseless planks of intellectual obstacles, and
Confront filtered daily blooming of correct doubtful
    Uncertain returning-
The most beautiful portrait of all-
Wardens wine death wiped to implore unsafe, sharpened,
And glazed as happy as the dime drenched sea;

Spiritual Stagnation (*cont.*)

Dusted off with a shrug of shade amongst an unstable
  Shuffle of never ending spectacle . . .

Drip

Savages, Flowers
Compassionate, begging to evaluate stale feeling
Floating metrical pattern
Cannot see to listen,
   Blind to what I hear-

Bleak and Stale
Despite the nostalgic appeal

The ever expanding mind
The pretension and provincial outlook you left behind
When you first fell to the feet of the bitter taste,
Of the dancing gel on your tongue; beginning to baste-

Your sedative,
Got you wasted-
Your down never been so high
But you're grounded,
Until tomorrow-
Wake into the eyes of the capsuled-gelled crystal lie...

Wake to find
A furrowed mind
Closed eyes and an angry heart that never heals

Drip (*cont.*)

Liver swells,
  But what the hell
All is well
Until the other kidney fails . . .

Biting Words

Words that bite
Like shears that snip
Drowning in the fluid of your fingertips

Gasping for a grasping, they slowly flail
Slice up the momentum with a charred thought nail

Broken, brittle;
Still the package protrudes
Slip, slid-
My ears 'round the heel of your boots

The albatross I wear,
I swear
Around my neck-
My tongue touched death
Slip your fingers up into forever's last breath

Slide your toes through my hair,
    With your lower lip underwater-
Lie first;
You know the truth,
    But why bother?

What was loose to my dick-
Was tight to my fist...

Put her first on my 'To Do' list . . .

Dancing Swallow of Eternity

Baptized in bong water
Problems aren't solved or explained-
They're magnified; mythified
Problems of life, evolution, and the stigma of existence
The flexing muscle of Faith embraces the entheogen,
   Ever-knowing, untenable and completely unnerving
   Divine inebriant...
The deep eyes and hearts of universal, prolific, sacred
   And provincial holiness-

That ideal moment,
When the sun and moon are in the same sky
Like one slid up on the other while sleeping-
And you stand nipple deep in the Pacific,
   Shivering off of your shoulders,
   Fear's icy veneer-
Lying breathless in the trusting, salty, buoyant hands
   Of the Sea;
Fast becoming the tiny cell of Oceana in your cupped
   Hands, that rapidly sift through the bottomless cracks
   Of your apologetic, fragile fingers...
Ones that once could drown an entire stream of thought
In one Dancing Swallow of Eternity;

Dancing Swallow of Eternity (*cont.*)

In an instance;
It was gone,
   From all the lives you left your mark upon...

Whisk and flail the palms of Hades,
   With the squirming toes of clarifying onlookers;
Caress of the smothered, snarling shards of glass...
Plucked and squeezed of the most violent choir chamber
   Of pursed lips;

Pinching the eyelids into fists...
Without guilt of mutinous conduct-
... the sequin crown of thorns you've ordered for the
Resurrection is on the way . . .

II.
The Black Tooth Shield of Invincibility shrouds the
   Virtue of impending time-
Like a stagnant, but lurking inoperable tumor at the base
   Of your spine-

Soft, weary moans-
Now, subtle as Earth tones...

Dancing Swallow of Eternity (*cont.*)

Dismissed and shrugged off as easily as the stalactites
   Of napalm;
Dripping off the jungle rot in the head of the acid
   Soldier still fighting in Vietnam...

III.
In the mineral mirror
I see my horns are appearing
And it's creeping, and the warmth is nearing

Disturbingly Beautiful;
   Charmingly Grotesque...

Once I thought I was wrong;
I was mistaken-

Diluted Truth of You

The most primitive and effective torture device is the
   Human memory-
Looking back on the memories of time well spent;
Contemplating the things I haven't done yet;
Meditating the time that came and went...
Chasing the blue skies off into the pores of forever . . .

Truth tends to evaporate and hide under the intense,
   Constricting light of investigation;
Addiction is good in moderation-
Momentary lapse of sedation...

This is what lies in the bowels of what war is made from
Pain tied to your years of lies
Darkness' brutal beating now due-
That is the Diluted Truth of You-

If once I tried,
Too many times
You wonder and ask why I lied...
Woke up still scheming
The cuspid, the wrinkle;
That keeps it all in
The PH is just right

Diluted Truth of You (*cont.*)

Do you implore?
Before,
It's completely forgotten-

Either stand up for something or sit the fuck down
No words have ever spoken more true-
That is the Diluted Truth of You-

Revelations on the Hindsight of the Yuletide

...Throughout some twist of fate, Western society has come to regard
dogmatic faith as a virtue.
To hold an idea as true, despite all evidence to the
   Contrary, is an abduction of reason.
Convictions are the end of knowledge,
   Not the beginning;
They are the Enemy of Truth more than that of lies

(12-25-01 – 11pm/EST)

Gone. . .

...As sobriety returns and the feeling of insight fades,
   one is left staring vacantly into the threshold of
   disjointed malignant phases.
One stares at a cadaverous-looking snow peak from
   Which Sunset has just fled-
That is the momentary birth of Consciousness;
The sobriety that offers no parallel-
Like a chronic, chemical pneumonia
Stricken to the restricting tether of the Mothership
Whatever that is;
No longer roaming in uncharted space of the unbecoming,
   Unknown curiosity-
No longer . . .
.. awakened to
...aware of

Revelations on the Hindsight of the Yuletide (*cont.*)

...embraced by
A new enlightenment -
  Poised for soul Evolution

Too Late to Blackout

You forget the pain, when you fly for a while
But every time you do, you die for a while

You try to hide, but the scar's inside
You can't breathe new life into a soul that's died–

  Rest
  The anger fed
  Once the fuel
   For all the hate you bred

How can You Prevail?
When you entrust in a God that Failed?

  You spin around, but it's too late to blackout
  You spin around, but it's too late to blackout

Battle of death, ends when you die
The one who survive, are the ones who cry–

Forgive me for what I've done-
So I can move on-

  You say you're out of tune with me...
  Maybe you're just on the wrong frequency—
All my life, I've been cheating . . .

Shit - Pig

Raining fragile tears of your god
Dripping Satan's semen de Sade

My blind bullet rips the saviour's flesh
Immortalized - thru your mortal eyes
That's the best I get–

Eyes are floating in a pool of angry tears
Lying helpless in a dermal layer of the
    Earth's crusty barrier

II.
Certainly looks pruvious today
Cumulus skies in my way
Already dreading the day
And I haven't got out of bed yet...

Born to fail
Never to prevail
What feeds and fuels this dilemma?
Fruits to horns, that scorn all odds
They soon run back to haunt us . . .

Phallic Didactic

He should know these Pacific Island streets
Silent as hip pockets;
Tight, Stuffed and widening
It's phallic didactic
Even the party doesn't rock the boat, Skipper
Even on board, you drown
Feet planted in the oarlocks and striking the
   Tide's dilated rise-
In vulgar reigning, circling attempts
Stomp until it hurts your feet,
   Prepare for everyone's alienated incarceration
Distorted,
In charge and motivated more than you could
   Ever conceive . . . ever

How could a routine not get sick?
Like rolling hills, days frolic steadily
Trembling along waves, take hold of the break
Before it's too late
Stride cracked and vulnerable
Hiding from change
Be neglected, Be afraid

You can't see it, but you hear it
In stereo orgasm, you're very near it–

Silvertigo

Times of crushed, pollen accented veils
I peer ugly and confidently upon waiting
    Fourth tier optimism
The kind that smears and smothers all ghetto
    Reason and why you are there in the third place-

Bronze and wooly
Breezy and adopted to my newly fingerprinted
    Eyebrow Lexi
Raised to kill eight beleaguered research violators,
    And addicts of syntax armory drug lord Cubanos-

Whom, now a sincere nod to femininity and hot-
    Bedded, sweet futuristic arrogance...
Quaint
Bloody, snot knuckled nostrils siphon the swollen
    Holy tongue-suppressed jerked final tear

Sold you my Volatile Ego

Sold you my volatile ego
I'm flowing over the equator,
   Where the doldrums aren't dormant
Ice caps and glass maps
Smooth around your lips
You stare off into something that seemingly is
   Not there ...

Pick up the pace
It's not a race
To some,
   Everything is heading nowhere

Innocence is anything but anal
Pestilence is found inside us all
Running narrow statements down the
   Flaccid limber hall
Beat on senseless proper attitude adjusted them all
It's standing;
Circling amarillo retinal glare on brown reclined
   Unjust empathy
Softly, singing, sweetly
Impoverish stream up seems to cross cut bending;
Green, blurry and bleak
Intrudes, so very eroding-

Asleep;

Sold you my Volatile Ego *(cont.)*

Pulled apart at apertures unheard of
Under rayon-marked rainy tiered agony
Spinning, Jagged Stars
   Knurled to grasp tips to frottage
Cease the search party for lost intention
I need it again–

What could disturb the still (ness)?
Riots at rest (lessness)?
Something will...
(Dean is such a fucking pessimist)

Don't roar back now,
It's all to disturb
Smash myself into a small, undiscoverable,
   Fragile tunnel leading to . . .
(Someone is coming...finally)

Got to Die, or You'll Live to Regret It

Fireworks, even when doused with copious amounts
  Of ethynol, don't seem to do it anymore...

Banging heads with corporate structure and
  Mechanical lifelessness;
Rotted and Rowdy
Universally irrelevant and unsubstantial

When you pass thru the portal and into the next
  Chamber of life, if there is one,
Be ready to go thru the Gauntlet once again–

My belief system and thought process is a work
  In a process of progress - constant evolution -
From the cradle to the grave,
The womb to the urn-

Cut clean the bindings of existence as we presently
  Know it, and vow to never again let a clinging or
  Suctioning action (vacuum) me into another
  Suffocating tank of Sweltering sorrow and
  Dysfunction...
I won't have it-

True truth lies within,
And it's true;
Lies are within the Truth

Got to Die *(cont.)*

No need for institutionalized religion to 'discover'
  Our own guidelines (god-lines?)
They keep us from realizing our true, undissolved
  Nature-

Love, Forever, Forgiveness, Healing, Miracles...
ARE in our power supply to realize-

When you ascribe to a higher being, you thereby
DENY your own power-

We are only limited by our own awareness and it is
  Expandable; Infinite

[what we chose one moment determines what we
  Are presented with in the next...?]

They want the control
Religion is the ultimate crowd control for the
  Fragile minded
When we discover our own true transcendent nature,
  We become harder to control

When you look out past yourself,
Way past and into the unknown, uncharted safe zone
It gets alluringly-fucking-frightening
Yin and Yang and the Tao theory is misbalanced

Got to Die *(cont.)*

Cosmic depressive,
Plastic, Robotic world outside of our own . . .

Mistakes are lessons taught,
Success is a lesson learned-

Tweak the reality frequency,
    To be more conducive to fit you
Pay more attention to those neglected or
    Outrightly ignored Pods-

Don't wait in line,
To lose your mind
Rush in like the rest of us ...

Got to Die or You'll Live to Regret It

Believing the absolute untenable is
    Completely unnerving
Like the impersonable god that can't be experimented directly . . .

Agenda of Gabionade

I have got to learn to give and not to take
That's a mistake I always make
When you cringe, you frown
Shows your concern, shows you're down

I was too high to take care of what was occuring
Everyday we see clearly,
Yesterday's things that once seemed so blurry

Wonder to our selves, Awaken to wonder
Plunder to depths, Abhorrent to be under
All the smiles and frowns, till it drags me down

We tell lies quietly
Truth's ears are listening;
Attentive to what we are saying-

Deep sea diving into the depths of inner space
   Throughout el dia
Processing at h-a-l-f speed, the theory of
   'Panspermia'
Do you sentence the homeless man to house arrest?
If you must...
And when you own a piece of land, do you own it all
   the way to the Earth's crust?

Apocalyptic Drug March

...a cellular and molecular approach to the functions
  of the nervous system...

It's Monday
Gulp down your good-morning Prozac with your
  Latte' Grande
Push and Turn
The sinister solution lies just below a layer of
  Puffy cotton and a child proof cap;
Pop three and take a long nap-

You take the hit (bump - bump- bump)
  without dreaming,
Or at least remembering what you dreamt

Cut yourself on the glass
But don't cut up my glass
Jesus Christ Almighty, my ass
If it were, you would surely do something about
  This shit
...short fall when you're crawling
...hard to hit bottom when you're already down
...only way is up when your lying on the ground

You tell me you're doing fine
As you rail up another line
Surely a sign;
Ignoring the beast you refuse to leave behind . . .

Pecuniary Diluvium

An entire decade is collapsing into the pill form
Killing Satan and logic
Making the user paranoid and psychotic
Playing neurochemical roulette with
    The irrefutable dimension of hell

Underground, steaming streams of Sulfur
10,000 degrees;
Heat that could turn iron to ashes
The bitter molten lake navigated by demons in
    Infernal canoes row defiantly on...

Boils your brain and reduces it to paste;
Full of hate, but none goes to waste-
Frozen fires burn bright,
Like the crown of Light
Placed around your head like a sedative halo-

Lightning's ragged teeth unzip a tattered denim sky
Cast out the lepers and welcome the demons with
    Open, loving thighs;
Ignorant, misinformed, vicious conversations medicate, but none the
fewer
As efficient as a dyslexic engraver,
Like cultivating a fucking sewer . . .

Epitaph (for lighthearted death)

The tombstone is in the shape of a giant
  Middle finger with an epitaph that says;
"Don't put your flowers on me when I'm dead
  Give them to someone who can smell them instead"

Clock has struck the 13th hour;
  The suffering power
You will have died a terrible death of pain and burn
  In the fiery, sweet trenches of hell forever they
  Say...

All the sleepless (t)weekends
You'll get all the sleep you need now

Prozac is no solution for your depressive ills-
A bunk, purple placebo;
  Another useless pill-

Gods of Steel await your arrival
The morbid revival
Scream you bastard Scream
The shrinking Violet, whithered;
Sucking slowly back into her roots
Cultivating the scene of the last sticky dream...

Shards of Inspiration

Lean over and hunker into the dust
If you must
The excavation of the inhalation of the ultimate
    Lack of care...
The narrow splinter of ambition, inspiration and
    Inevitable despair-
You're there . . .

Art of Shit Art

So you sit and face the wall
Do you recognize me?
Speak to me . . .
Say you're clawing for the words

My tears creep down
  And try to avoid you
Did you notice?
Cause now you're crying too...

Wouldn't it hurt to know?
Sitting across from you...
Staring right thru...
Thinking of her

Your callous heart,
  Doesn't scab anymore
Bruised, scraped and battered
It will never break again-

At least, not for me

Tuesday I Think...

The worst bar I've ever been to...
No, the liquor wasn't bad,
   The way they poured or mixed it-
This bar in Long Beach

I sat there and watched myself
That crab red face and those pale hands,
Through a well mirror in front of me
And I watched the metamorphic change...

A near hung-over man,
Losing color, turning grey
Now glowing crimson at eight a.m.

I hate this fucking bar...

I stayed there until one-thirty p.m.

All day...

Hating it . . .

[M]ass-inine

Crippled minds, you think alike
Hobble off to your spoon-fed life

Tired and worn teachings of the cross you serve
But to preach to me,
Pre-packaged ideas; what nerve...

You stare at me as if it's *my* soul that is lost
You pay for your tuition each Sunday
How much did that cost?

You quote from a book that has no author
To secure a place in heaven, I say ' why bother?'

Weak minds, you think alike
Cause your ideas are tunneled thru the pastor's mic

The organized propaganda you fuckers cast
Is the one I point my finger at...

So gather in your "A" frame,
That you paid to build
Fill it to the cap, Fill it to the hilt

Close the door, and close your mind
Leave your individuality behind...

[M]ass-inine *(cont.)*

They manipulate and strip your head...

'You know when you reach out for something that
has already grabbed hold?'

Sink Like a Stone

Success results in excess
Beast's belly hits the bone
Down on your own
Alone
Left to sink like a stone

Trials are miles as they past
Smiles are weary, not to last

The sweet is all bitter
And all things considered
The duller the conviction
Less apphrehensive;
Contradictive

The groans and moans
Now subtle as earth tones
The bird has been flown, on its own

The weight of the world on your shoulders
As Atlas only can
Be that man
Goddamn
Standing in quicksand
Once again
Alone;
Left to sink like a stone

Seraglio

You say it's good
I want to try it
You say, ' too much of this shit will kill you'
Maybe you just need more bourbon in your diet

Plunge head first
Your ass is the last one out
Making sure, there ain't no doubt
About it…

Cars hiss by
Hurts too much to piss
But I'll try
Lost, unwanted and they don't need us
Discarded like an aborted fetus

Plausible Fingering

U play me to the point of bullshit
U can't wait to cluster-fuck my day
U patronize this game as if it were your own
   Demise and not my own...
U wait for my respect,
   You haven't earned-
U contemplate our fate,
   You'll never learn-

I say whatever;
Never
Turn my grey shroud into clever
You sever
Any and all points of the Great Hate
Stick your fingers at me,
Tell me to die,
Can't wait . . .

You suffer thru me
I make you hate, you say
Feels much too easy to anger you,
Don't loathe me that way

The nightmare I see; Me
The demon you call on to fuck
I'm writing the soundtrack to a Down-

Plausible Fingers *(cont.)*

You drown
Frown;
Upon me and my ways-

Keep smiling,
You got to-
They'll know otherwise then,
That they got U . . .

II.

She hung up on me when I called her 'drunk'
No, no, I was drunk...
I called her, '_____'

I wonder what I said . . .

Maximum Meandering

Torque the chasm;
Crank thru bottomless spiral nostril flow
Geeked the fuck out on shitty-ass'd
   Buckhead blow
You know?
And whose nose?
That always knows...
Look out below!

Morning gagger hit heavy on the larynx pit
Shake it off,
Rattle spilled and ticked mine off,
And that's it-
Or some shit
Is that enough?
Too much?
Tough . . .

I do a line
You do a line
No, not that kind-
-that leaves you broke and partially blind
You stiff the prophets,
You quote Nostradamus,
You lie in the wake of this counter moon,
   As the stars look down upon us-

Maximum Meandering *(cont.)*

I throw the switch-
As the sick bastards twitch-

Brand me with the scars that never heal
Too real...
Now I conceive grouted lies
   on the fly-
Living just to die
Makes you just want to cry-

Can you wait for the flood?
Too much mud-
To wade thru-
   -the shit
I'm standing in

Staring up into Port side
Glide step-right up into the earlobe
   Of the hypocrite
Nice fit
What's become of it?
The concrete ricochet...
Reload, duck and hold
Put the fukn .22 away
(it's the deuce-deuce)
It's the stigmatic muse-

Maximum Meandering *(cont.)*

Low and behold
Loss of control
Hide in your Interpol
Back-up into destiny's death hole
   That has set aside the freaks from tyrants
Cultivated and Migrant-
  -farm plows
What's up now?

Face the Day
Abysmal tidal wave
Slave to your future grave
Sustain too much agony
You give up into viral triad enclaves . . .

Bite down and mulch the 1000 yard stare
But beware;
Ransack if you dare
Wonderlust resurrecion scare-

Enough to worry the sickest of dreamers
  -that never sleep and stay awake-
Riding thru the return of daylight's revenge and
   Too much at stake-
To fake
Scavenger lost sailing the crimson lake

Maximum Meandering *(cont.)*

Dry, arid and baked
A single grain of faith-
Sand, Sediment and Flake

Wishing
Hoping-
Praying-
Searching to Prey

Meat-hook reality curls into the flesh of Today . . .

Torrid Holiday Tomorrow Comes

Inn
That Hell
I say, 'Farewell'

You wonder why doors are locked,
   And if too much of this shit will someday
   Kill you...

Of course, you know that...
If rampant,
   You dwindle all existing metaphor...

My eyes are closed
But I know I need a refill when my brow touches
   The other-side of the Green Mug...

I wake up from not-sleep with eyes like China;
Very close to closed
Hesitant to accept the confronting day...

We're an hour past check-out
   And I can't drive-

Fuck it...
Tell 'em we're staying another night-
Cut up another line, I'll get more ice . . .

Rostrum Debris Havoc

Standing on the front of the stage,
The band blackened and looming in the background-
So many lights
Angles piercing through me;
Penetrating, and leaving me vulnerable
Can you have useless talent?
You can,
    And I'm in abundant possession-

The knight kneeled,
    And that's where it ended
Awake;
Trying to remember...

II.

" I will continue my drinking binge"
He did sigh his cringe-
And on he strolled...

...motivated to swallow
Hollow man's dream and hopes of dilemma
And off he drank-
And walked the plank;
For the last time;
    off the room window of the Super 8 . . .

Igneous Pulchritude

I sat and watched the fucker drop from the top of
  The closet to the floor,

I watched him crawl;
Around, looking for a cavern to crawl into-

Then I started to think...

Think of the way people look for a second or two
  At that spider or insect crawling on the wall-

Bewildered;
Lost;
Scared-
And suddenly smash it with a shoe or open hand

I think...

Then I lash out and kill the fucker myself-

Now I really start to think . . .

7 a.m.

The last face I want to see, at times.
At times, the demon I can't bare to look at;
At times, the most angelic visage I can't wait to
   Come home to-
That beast continues to pour and drain;
Into the glaciered glass and the life out of me-
Dis-respectively...

Don't want to possess sick serpent fingers
Ran into the narrow appearing, conjuring horns-
Grasped, Embraced all domains
Took only what I confess to be piercing and
   Appealing to me
Blessed sacred, scarred channels
Humbled in rusted, modest extravagance

In the early hours,
   When I would arrive
Sunrise;
Clear, concise, quiet and alive-
Outside and in my head,
   I now realize

Turn down streets I've never been on and say
   I used to live there-
And now you know I used to fake those heart
   Attacks;

7a.m.(Cont.)

Clutch my chest and bulge out my eyes
Now you laugh;
You don't scream or cry;
Anymore

I would find it extravagant to be in a pageant
A dereliction of obscenity;
A calling to serenity
Too fond of markings,
Plagued on journey's swollen embarkings
Flailing ignorant abduction,
    Pulled into groping bosom seduction
The suction;
Now deemed a luncheon-

Echo head;
Rabbit smitten crash
Levitating, stumpy escort;
Pocket margin cohort
Treasure, trailer transpositional trash
I think I would just die instead-

I got a hang-up
It's a phobia
Not a labia,
    And not utopia
I'm into smokestack,

7a.m. (cont.)

Not refutable,
Not inscrutible,
Just gratuital

Indulge in priveledge;
   Proceed to pillage
Tempt magenta, and encrypt the message-
All join to ransack,
The safe - cracker
The gun-packer
The car-jacker
Today, we will all learn
To burn the urn, we are gonna live forever
   or learn to earn;
Courts adjourned . . .

Election Day

The 74 year old senator from Nebraska doesn't
  Slam smack or snort blow-
But he does drink Johnnie Walker Red
He won't ever smoke a joint,
But will continue to inhale two packs of Camels
  A day until he's dead-

...She said, ' Have a drink before I tell you this...'
I had three and still wasn't ready-

She used to always come up and visit me
They all did...
Half squinted, staring at the small creature in my
  Shorts next to me
Sweaty and flush from the drive-

When the room stopped throbbing and I was now a
  Dripping, dehydrated mess;
I wanted to go to work

Waiting,
Waiting,
8am
At home amongst the cacti, desert heat and the shit
  On the counter;
Waiting for me like a worried parent . . .

Wisdom, Grasshopper. . .

For a roll of pennies,
   It costs you a buck-
Sprinkle all one hundred throughout your day
Imagine;
Giving one hundred people good luck. . .

...Or

Fold it in half length-wise and put it in her
   garter belt...
In one hundred years,
Who's gonna give a fuck?

Dust Cloud

Always waiting
Sitting around waiting
Waiting for something;
The phone, the door, an impulse, an urge...

I sit, staring into the stereo
Losing for a moment the thought of death and the
    Dormant state...
I take a huge inhale and the flood of the good,
    Long, drink
I recline and stare at the ceiling...
Waiting-

II.
I think they are getting wise to my demise
At the least,
    Ripe for the picking...
I loaded the blue and red bag for the weekend
Destination?
I'm gone....
Fuck the bag.
I'll buy a shirt when I get there
Where?
Don't know, but will when I arrive
Is there an ATM?
How much will I need?
(all of it)

Dust Cloud *(cont.)*

...this is going to be a fucking heavy one...

III.
You dictate me
You poison your enemy
Now you dissolve the lie
Open wide;
No reason to live
A million to die
A new bottle, two pills and a vile
   The reasons multiply
Stiff as wire
With your blood on fire
Shooting and shaking
'But what you making?'
An honest man a liar?
Fistful of excuses
From lame to pondering
Analyzing is an excuse,
    In case you were wondering...

IV.
I awoke to a golden sword of light
I craned my neck over my right shoulder,
   Squinting deliberately into the blinding view-
Tearing and blinking, I rise...
An omen?

Dust Cloud *(cont.)*

A journey to religious expressive outlets unknown?
My sandals are still on my socked feet
I peer into the green to see a mound of half melted brown ice...

I stumble to my feet
I open the door slowly as the bright, white light
   Finds my eyes
Hallelujah!
Silver and intrepid it stares at me with reluctance
   To be conquered
But I'm done with it in one long, prolonged
   Swallow

Eyes closed
Gripped to the counter top
Hoping today;
Good news will come my way . . .
I'm waiting-

Precious Dregs

There is nothing pressing I want
I miss wanting
I miss striving
I've obtained it...
The things I Attacked, embraced and went for
They are mine and it's bullshit...

I miss wanting
I want what's missing...

An undaunted, relentless pursuit of extremity
A slow, transitory capitulation of exhorbitant
    Quantities of distilled earth
Encircle the cessation as if dredding the entire
    Current experience-
Prolonged numbness and isolation of belief and
    Senses;
Fear and hostile disappointment...

Will it hurt?
Apparently...
Pushing insanity
A great surge,
    A reflective, feeling lurking
The correct angle foreshadows-
I already know, and it disgusts and abhors me
A slave to my self in a fully engulfed,

Precious Dregs *(cont.)*

Consciously
Languid trance...aware of it now

II.

Flying first class
Best shit you can buy
No not the grass-
Take a hit
Too many roots have been smoken'
No jokin', tokin' stinks
Whatever happened to free drinks?
It's too late to scruffle over details...
Scar -faced rock chicks
Nothing surrendered to slouching in the bar end,
     My friend...

III.
Scared to live
Scared of living
Scared of what I've become,
     Scared of becoming-
Bury the dead
Bury the dying
Bury the alive,
     The ones who've stopped living . . .

This is What Screams are Made of...

Flight 314

The crows make clatter and strut the curbline
Fat bodied,
Full of thrown-back street trash and fresh carrion
Pecking away at the eyes of fallen street life
Like urban Vultures;
They wade in the cultivated sewers of the City
Knawing and tearing...

The sky looked unpleasantly disturbed,
   Dinged alongside the horizon
Rancid, grey clouds;
Faltering and shredded,
Seemingly by the swift, agile claw of the Bengal
Long, slender slices of Sunshine confidently
   Stride thru the apertures of intruding blue sky...

II.
Stone Grey Eyes

   You get the strangest, most vile looks from the elderly sometimes.
Not the quiet ones that pass you with an approving smile and are
seemingly, vicariously living thru you. But instead, the bitter

old sots that presumably skipped something or missed out on their
descent into obscurity. Damn shame put on them for not living and
enjoying their tenure of youth on the planet. Here's to them, for
further dulling the tarnish of their 'Golden Years'.

If for once,
True majestic buoyance of reason would surface
Infuriated, teary-faced snide remarks of the defeated;
The inferiority complex addled Legions of nervous
    Onlookers,
Dangerous treachery of the mass bombardment of
    Senile virility...

Sanctioned, Misguided Abundance of once ugly Clobbering of semi-
medicated Emotion...

III.
Eight Miles High

Time doubled in the space vacuum
Almost indigenous to the unadulterated, bad luck
    Wondering of the untethered conventional
    Thought process...
...like staring at a swollen picture on ground level
    dope deals gone terribly wrong
Target moving sunrise smitten with sweaty palmed
    Travellers-

What Screams *(cont.)*

IV.
And the Plane Also Rises...

At 15,000 feet,
    Grey mountaintops are undistinguishable from
    Fast approaching once-distant clouds
Your lungs lunge and shrink into safe harbors in
    Your hollow-cored torso
Depth perception is now panoramic
Look to the sky;
Inside
That is where you are to hide
Too much contemplation;
Worry and contemplation
The lonely death contemplates;
Contemplating the Death
Bowing out,
    You poor, sick bastard...
Toning and conditioning
You snort and binge often enough that your
    Eyeballs suck into the middle of your skull
There is enough repitory, vacuuming torque to
    Plausibly sniff up a Honda Civic
A hatch-back of course
But let's conquer the conquesting moment for
    The moment...

What Screams *(cont.)*

Ignorant thoughts are flying thru an unforgiving,
    Misfortune of Tenacity...
In this City;
Where the doors slam shut as your engine screams
    Into consciousness and restlessly eases itself
    Into the traffic
Times tend to lend themselves into oozing multi-
    Hued masses of molded fiberglass and recycled
    Alloys...

At least at this elevation...
Far too much conflicting cross-rays and bolts of
    Cancerous Light Beams–
Flicker and Strut with laser precision
Deadly at this altitude
Cruel and Demeaning...

V.
JUNGLE MUSIC DOWN WHERE THE
    'CLOSED EYED' IS THE OCCASION-

One scream after another
The kind that curdles your cum
Makes you squint into the horizon
Straight into Daylight's long, winding grasp

What Screams *(cont.)*

And who forgave who?

You squeeze your eyelids Down to your Nostrils
    To cover the shrapnel rings
And things...

Maybe one day
We can all back our own egos into the Summit and
    Stomp lightly on marked memories Past;
A dangerous wish
At last
Gasp!
A solemn grasp,
    At the past....

VI.
Lip Service

A lifetime later,
We touch down-
A complete stranger to the shackled, shadowed
    Man in chains of trickery below
This, I hope, will be of opulent strength and
    Undiluted perseverance of the diminishing
    Faith in the Shrouded goodness of Humanity-

What Screams *(cont.)*

The Column rose from the rubble of the
    Fallen shadows
Crumbled into dust;
Like the deteriorating, humanitary-faith in Reality
Our perception of hair-triggered annihilation and
    Utter contempt of the Dissolving Isolation of
    All American Dreams...
Forever and Ever...Amen...
No
Not yet...

VII.
...This is What Screams Are Made Of ...

I'm dying toWin
I'm living toLose...

We grounded with a thud
Silenced with a firm bellow
Sit tight now, and do your best for the prep of
    Death
Don't look now-
Here Comes!!!
Put and keep your tray tables in their full, upright,
    And locked position...

VIII.

Bodacious Cowboys

I stagger off the aircraft
Dragging my carrion (carry on ?)
   Reluctantly behind me
I begin to yell for no foreseen reason
Who Cares Wins?

Exactly …

Thorns of Hope

This fucking cursor is blinking at me again tonight
This last night
As usual,
I have nothing to say to it...
It just blinks...
I misspell words and can't express the other ones
    Properly...

And what the fuck over?
Is it really worth it?
The cohesiveness of that strain of doing my
    'Destiny thing' is so strong
It dictates my life
My whole adult life...
Always has....
And I guess it should-

I've learned thru time to forgive
But nothing can erase completely-
No matter how thin the membrane,
    Or translucent the tissue gets,
You can't forget
Scarred like the cut on your arm,
Until you parish-

Thorns of Hope *(cont.)*

Those eyes
Those Bombastic, Sinister, Prying, Cold Bulbs
The ones in the steel reflection every morning
Those are the killer;
The ones that you cannot slip up in front of...
Violent rush to the senses soon to follow-

When the talking turns to noise;
    And the paranoia creeps in
Head in your Hands
The lies
The pain
Your face in the cocaine
You realize then,
    You have returned worse than ever...

... Looking to circle HOPE in the want ads...

Lying in the kitchen and mumbling about how the
    Linoleum looks like it was actually based on an
    Ancient hieroglyphic sent forth from the Greek-
    God Hermes...

I can see how you can lie to me
But how can you lie to yourself?
Should I be left alone?
Can't replace me when I'm gone...

Thorns of Hope *(cont.)*

Push and turn
2-3 a day
Now 5 an hour
You'll learn...

I concepted and conceived
And gave birth to a dream
Or did the dream have me?

Downloading ideas as freely as beads thrown off
    The balconies on Rue Bourbon Street-

Wall dripped and rolled in shadowed waves;
As the drapery did its wiggle next to an open window;
The lonely candle dripped its molten, purple til
    It dried up into hard little buttons on the
    Smoking, Bombay table of redwood...

.... The Sheer weight of thought and the gravity by which I see reality...

Tinseled down and cascading the ice and defrosting
    The windshield on a cold Hades morning-
I FELL INTO THE THORNS OF HOPE.
I BLED . . .

Last Voice Lost

An enema done up erotically
Right here in Big Time Nowhere, U.S.A.

It's organic;
It's in our metabolism;
Hard to digest, but shits out the same
It's trancendance

Consistently Unpredictable philosophy,
    Dressed up as a really bad joke-

Valium, Crown and a life full of letdowns
    Come screaming out the vacuum tube
Hotter than an L.A. crackpipe on welfare day
Or that thick and enriched vile of 'K'
That burns your drip and steals your soul
As you operate your body by remote control,
    While seemingly looking through a fishbowl...

A Rope Ends it = Desperation

Dilated Peoples perch atop our missle silo,
   Hovering above the warhead like a doomsday halo.

Consequences of truth's disembowelments
You think I'm sick as I sprinkle them with arsenic
It's a completely anonymous situation,
   But you feel inclined to make some sort of impression
Twisted and sick you feel the resurrection of synthetic depression
And here's the lesson...

You came into the cab smelling like deodorant, toothpaste, and
   Perfume.
You fall out 5 hours later smelling like vomited alcohol, garlic
   And cigarettes.
In no particular order, but I digress...
The thick, rich, nauseating stink of momentary happiness

Ass strapped onto the business end of an atomic bomb
Ready to blow to Kingdom Come Along
In the basement, the children pull the wings off of flies
And before they can jump, the angels are stripped of theirs
Beware;
Face the rap, the endearing trap
You crawl and sniff around
All the cavernous cracks in this town

They are dropping the 500 pound kaboom drums from 5 miles high
A thousand times a day and continue to climb
Were in the trenches and foxholes,
   Sniping one pilot at a time
That's progress, but again, I digress...

Ronson Award

Axis II personality disorder coupled with the vaunted apocalyptic
  Coal – fired ebony heart attack
Burns black as ash
Rare red meat and sour mash
Torrential downpour of biblical proportions
Eternal mysteries of the psyche and the dark truth about abortions
Ones that float helpless in our dreams of unredeemable fears

Stretch the weekends as far as we can
Lives we breathe into and ones we smother
Give up one vice and get hooked on another

Living on a binge
Crooked spoon and a syringe
Breathe deeply
What is that smell?
They say you can't live what you can't inhale…

Addiction is a need (Don't buy it)
Affected is a want (Want to try it?)

If a thought crossed your mind, it would be a slow and lonely journey

The Anti-Social Drinker

...Enhance food
Enliven the mind,
Lubricate conversation,
Enrich life;
Drunkeness will come they say.

Well, they also say love is the devil whose boots you lick
Venom lips wrapped tight around your intellect
Faded, scarred tissue of your shedded skin
Trading up your horns for a halo again-

Got to step on a few toes to get where you are going
When anger is brewing and the blood alcohol content is growing

The Paraclete stands and you fall at its feet
Palaver begins and the squeeky wheel gets the grease
Complaints-
The true lubricant of the preservation of democracy
Toccata of hypocrisy
Reparations of mutinous conduct and objective probing
That is textbook complacent, sinister policy

Damaged Baggage

Excess baggage on a dead man's hand
Hard hearted
Confined, state of mind

In deep, for now
All I can remember
Can't sleep
Want to celebrate the season

Spent the post day with a face I adore
3 years ago seems like the day before

Sun melted into the horizon,
    And swallowed up the reminents of the last day before departure
Sucking the lost blue barrier out of the tiny brazen retinal path
A maelstrom of synthetic math
Catholics kill the Protestants
Jews kills the Palestineans
You blink, trip and spill the ink
As all the world is now riveted to the canvas where the
    Splash made a dash and the spot made a dot

"It embodies the center of the universe"

"It's the embryo of the woman's womb before evolution"

That's what they are saying, and with no complaints
You nod and for the first time in the history of modern man,
    We all agree. Everyone.

Ultimate Groove Cushion

Success turns to excess
A lie without a liar
Staggering thru life
Tripping over discarded dreams and spilt drinks

Group shots amount to the thought of being there
    To look back on and smile
Even though, you know, they will soon be left alone
In a box,
Long after you are gone;
Slowly fading and dying and turning to dust themselves

I wanted to fly
You said I could
I wanted to die
You said I should
The best advice is often times misleading

Effigy

Lemmings rush to the sea
As moths to the light
You run for the door
You run for your life

Deep sea diving into the depths of inner space;
Vast, lonely plains with no rolling, lofty hills in its topography;
An empty savannah that melts into a fast sinking sunrise;

The distant and gentle symphonic siren song of suicide
And the times we tried
And the ones who died

Palanquin

Reaccess this nervous breakdown
Dullest stars shed the blackest light-
Internal fortresses are damned
Ash painted hearts and encrypted closed-eye insight

The sweet sucking off of Fall's steep festival
Regripped what was slipped out of an eyebrow's grasping trite testicle
Once hollow men;
Now filled to the brim with him
Cozy martyr fucked silly
Eaten alive by the HIV slim-

Postpartum Postponement

A cloud, cloaked moon
Like the ones seen on covers of novels about the occult...

I want to be sprinkled across the ocean
Spread my ashes among the sea
Spend my days in the doldrums
Spend my nights in the feverish hands of the last deity

I wake to find
A vacancy by my side
Glad to know
You left last night

Slither up the bicep of life
Christ;
An inch off the top would be nice
Sick to slam
Face to slap
Gave away a dozen to get one back-

Brides dream
Disabled pet
I think about you all the time
How I wished we never met-

I find you in the latrine
On your knees
Arms and head resting on the rim
I sit on the sink and drink
I recite poetry while you puke...

Requiem and Goodnight

It's the density
  That's creeping in on me
Lie back and close your eyes
What do you think about?
Death ...
Where you're going ...
Where you've been ...
Much to your chagrin

Hustlers and Whores
Coattails caught in rear car doors
No more
It's the fast dying to never end
Pressure comes down hard
You break before you bend

Out jumped the sinister urge
  In the fascade of a dirge
This surge
Energized while you wait
Your pushed into a bundle and
  Packed like freight

Scoldings over the Tulsa summit
  And your ribs protrude and shift with
  Violent pandemonium
Forgiven, but not forgot like shards of
  Lithium

Exeunt Wound Genesis
   (sing you obese bitch)

I've once again reached the bottom of yet another wicked one
The one that kills;
The one that heals;
The one that hunkers helplessly with uncertainty
My eyes close at last and there is the ubiquitous reform ...

The sting of a million illuminous cones and rods and spirals and curves
Incendiary revulsions like kerosene dreams;
     Fleeting and without time
Peels of undisturbed distilled windfalls
Descending to its impending magnificence
The final splintered, distraught thought ...

For once I believe
Now it's confirmed by the scarab
Snorting the final fragments from the urn
And the swallow and the burn

The sick heretic is beneviolent
And askewed
Ripe, twisted and overdue
The bruxism halts to a silent thud among the molars
     And awaits the bruised arid lips
Followed and hallowed by the passing of the accrid glottis glum

Simply just another depraved lie for a liar whose life has
     Been consumed
Naught remnants of ruin scatter like frightened field mice with
     Upturned nostrils and sordid, snorting rapture
Pungent with guilt;

This life
Right now
That is where it ends and how it dies
Beneath the pressurized shroud of murderous lies

I should be ashamed, but I am most ceremoniously not ...
Fall into the thorns and bleed.
Bleed you bastard, bleed ...
One last time for me.

JEW°

WAR! TERROR!

SEX! DISILLUSION,

DRUGS + DISFUNCTION

AND ALL OTHER THINGS

THAT MAKE THE

LIFE WORTH LIVING,

WHEN THE RESURRECTION

COMES, THERE

WILL BE A TWO

DRINK MINIMUM,

BRING ME A

DOUBLE—

PARTNERS IN THE

PERFECT CRIME,

KAM

Printed in the United States
16093LVS00001B/67-90